The
Kingdom
of the
Occult

Rev. Glenn T. Walter, M.ED., PH.D.

To order additional copies of this book contact:
Leadership Training Consultants, Ltd.
6500 Emerald Parkway
Suite 100
Dublin, Ohio 43016
614-493-8543

FWB

Columbus, Ohio

Dr. Glenn Thomas Walter has trained thousands and raised more than four million dollars to fund leadership training projects throughout the United States. His professional business expertise spans more than 25 years in both private and public sectors. He currently serves as President/CEO of Leadership Training Consultants, Inc., located in Columbus, Ohio. Additionally, Dr. Walter is the

Director of Servant Leadership Training at Trinity Lutheran Seminary and an academic fellow of Princeton Theological Seminary.

The first African American to serve as President/CEO of Columbus Works, Inc. a renowned Central Ohio employment training conglomerate nationally recognized for its "Best Practices" in occupational skills development and training. Columbus Works, Inc. was the first business in Ohio to receive such distinction in its industry. Dr. Walter has been invited to Washington D.C. on numerous occasions to present his distinctive and extraordinary processes to the United States Department of Labor's Effective Practices Panel (PEPNet) of employment experts. He is also an honored recipient of the prestigious Walter & Marian English Award presented by United Way of Central Ohio for outstanding contributions in social services.

WWW.DRGLENNWALTER.COM

DEDICATION & ACKNOWLEDGEMENTS

This project is dedicated to our Lord and Savior Jesus Christ. With Christ all things are possible to them that believe! I also want to acknowledge my family, staff and the host of volunteers that prayed and sacrificed to make this project possible. Lastly, I dedicate this work to the loving memory of my parents, Tom and Diane Marie Walter and Bishop Norman L. Wagner, my Spiritual Father.

INDEX

THE KINGDOM of the OCCULT
THE POWER of CHOICE

The occult is a rapidly growing global religious practice. Occult practices permeate every hierarchical echelon throughout human civilization. The origins of witchcraft, sorcery, mediums and soothsayers are as ancient as the first Mesopotamian civilization. People are captivated by supernatural activities for which there is no scientific explanation. We want the power to know what is unknowable. More specifically, the populace desires detailed information about its future (horoscope). Governments, especially those with religious rudiments that underscore its constitutional structure, covet the ability to influence the minds of its citizenry. It is our lust to know the unknowable and control what is uncontrollable that drives us to explore by any means necessary, including dark magic or occultism.

Regrettably, people think their right to know supercedes the need to obey God's Word. This is not a new human dynamic. Our adamic (sinful) nature compels us to question divine parameters. In other words, we want to test the boundaries of anything forbidden, especially if it has the potential to produce desired results. You may be wondering, why God allows people to make contradictory decisions. Good question. Why did God create people with the innate ability to flagrantly disobey His laws? The existential answer is known as choice.

God created us with the ability to make choices, even if those choices are contrary to His perfect will for our lives. What exactly is the perfect will of God for man? The Bible declares:

> "The Lord is not slow in keeping His promises, as some understand slowness. Instead he is patient with you, not wanting anyone to perish, but everyone to come to repentance."
>
> ~ 2 Peter 3:9

Therefore, we clearly understand that God desires that you "come to repentance." It is not God's will that anyone should perish. However, the Lord has given us the ability to choose. Let us explore the concepts associated with God's will/plan and human choice.

God's *"thelema"* (Will) and God's *"boulema"* (Plan) are fundamentally important words when discussing the issue of choice. The Greek word *thelema* is used about 60 times in the NT. It is usually translated "will." It denotes the desire or wish. However, the Greek word *boulema* refers to one's resolve. It goes beyond a mere desire. It denotes the actual plan, the intention, or the outworking of the will. God is sovereign, but by His sovereignty allows man to act in opposition to His *thelema* but not His ultimate *boulema*. Herein lies the impression of conflict between man's capacity to choose and God's divine preference. *Thelema* merely expresses choice (God's or man's), and in most cases can be translated properly as "will." Man, because of the authority granted to him over the earth, for a brief period is permitted to violate the will of God. Man, however, cannot violate God's predestined plan. God's predestined plan is His *boulema.* Understand that *boulema* has a predisposition for finality or "ultimate plan." From God's perspective, His *boulema* is inclusive of man's disobedience to His will.

For example, consider Eve's statement in Genesis 3:2-3: "The woman said to the serpent, we, may eat fruit from the trees in the garden, but God did say, you must not eat fruit from the tree that is in the middle of the garden, and you must not touch it, or you will die." It is obvious that Eve clearly understands God's mandate not to perform a particular act (eat a specific fruit). Nevertheless, Adam and Eve both ate forbidden fruit because God gave them the ability to choose (*thelema*). God created us morally free beings, capable of making decisions. We are free to choose right/good or wrong/bad. Without the element of choice, we are merely robotic creatures programmed to do whatever our Creator prescribes. Although, Adam and Eve choose poorly, it did not preclude God from unfolding His plan of redemption through Christ (*boulema*).

As Christians, we are instructed to refrain from participating in clandestine activities. The Word of God is replete with warnings about participating in sorcery, witchcraft, soothsaying or dark magic. Occult participants take tremendous pride in endeavoring to by-pass or "go around" God's power and form an alliance with the powers of evil in order to gain an advantage. The occult emphasizes the sacredness of "hidden knowledge." Christians should always avoid vowing oaths to spiritual societies or secret orders to gain knowledge (*See* Deuteronomy 18:10-12; Leviticus 20:27; Malachi 3:5; Acts 8:9-13; Revelation 18:23 and Revelation 22:15).

The Bible declares, "Now the Spirit [speaks] expressly, that in the latter times some shall depart from the faith, giving heed to seducing spirits, and doctrine of devils" (1Timothy 4:1). Occultism is a very sinful practice. It emphasizes an earthly and corrupt form of wisdom. Again, the Word of God, "This is not the wisdom that comes down from above, but is earthly, unspiritual, demonic" (James 3:15). The children of God secures wisdom from the Lord God (James 3:17).

As God's servant leader, I have labored under the inspiration of the Holy Spirit to present this project as a means of informing, persuading and encouraging. It is my pastoral assignment to escort captives to a sacred place of liberation through the power of Jesus Christ.

On behalf on my LTC, Ltd., staff and its volunteers, may God be exalted and many souls delivered through the influence of this project and power of Jesus' great name!

Advancing the Kingdom of God,

Glenn Thomas Walter
Servant Leader

7

The Beautiful Packaging of Bondage

- The word *occult* comes from the Latin word *occultus,* meaning hidden or secret things. Participation in the occult is to practice attaining supernatural knowledge or powers apart from the God of the Bible. Through these practices, occultists seek to influence the present or future circumstances of their lives or the lives of others.

- The Word of God defines the *occult* as having its origin with Satan, the devil: Satan is a malevolent spirit-being determined to steal, kill and destroy all people.

- Occultism often refutes and denies the Godhead, the deity of Christ. His atonement on the Cross for our sins, and His bodily resurrection, it also attempts to promote a convoluted blend of Christian and occult beliefs.

The early years of television sitcoms produced an adorable attractive young suburban wife who called upon spirits, spells, and magic to navigate day-to-day life. Her husband, a marketing executive, and cute little daughter were always safely protected from harm because of her powers as a witch.

Another generation was cleverly introduced to a seemingly harmless cartoon series of cute little blue characters that used their "good white magic" to defeat evil warlocks, spirits and pill-bottle demons. This loving blue clan of characters lived together in a wonderful village protected by magic. This Hanna-Barbera cartoon series has generated over 50 billion dollars worldwide. The merchandising includes: Ice Capades musicals, action figurines, book bags, purses, lunch boxes, music recordings, theme parks, food sales, clothing items, and games (board & electronic). Children were cunningly introduced to lovable blue witches and wizards that millions of parents found simply adorable.

Satanists are no longer masking their agenda through charming delightful cartoons. One children's sorcery movie series truly has an international appeal as readers in 200 nations, in over 40 languages, enjoy indulging in its characters boldly associated with witchcraft. One U.S. consumer research survey reports that "over half of all the world's children between the ages of 6 and 17 (est. 900 million) have read at least one book" appertaining to this series. Interestingly, the main character is a young teenage male who has been properly trained at the "School of Wizards and Witchcraft." With the financial backing of Warner Brothers, Mattel, Coca Cola, and Scholastic, Inc., this movie series and affiliated books will have an indelible impact on the minds of children for generations to come.

Such movies and television programs popularized the kingdom of the occult. The occult, however, is not new. It has thrived since the beginning of civilization. Throughout the Old and New Testaments, prophets and apostles of God confronted problems related to the occult. These holy servants did not find wizards, witches, or those with familiar spirits cute or loveable.

SECTION ONE
The Rationale for Involvement

The predominant reason for occult involvement is disillusionment with the church and its controversial practices. Secondly, teenagers and young adults are fiercely resistive to organized religion and its unfulfilling platitudes. The third factor is curiosity. There is an attraction to the occult that appeals to our interest in the supernatural. Others begin with "harmless" dabbling, but this often leads to a progressive search for more. Occult, like cult followers generally fall into distinct and descriptive categories. Some followers are composed of essentially normal people who turn to the supernatural in times of sudden loss, disappointment, or frustration of unfilled expectations. Margaret Thaler Singer, a California-based psychologist who has counseled hundreds of cult members, estimates that 75 percent are basically "normal."

[1]Boston psychiatrist Dr. John Clark, maintains that based on personal examination of people in all stages of cult involvement, about 60 percent are chronically disturbed and only 40 percent are essentially normal. The latter were susceptible to conversation either because of normal, through painful "cries of maturation," or because they could not withstand the pressure exerted on them by an aggressive proselytizer. Another category of cult followers is made up of people who have shown considerable evidence of developmental and emotional problems over an extended period of time. They have been described as "searchers or seekers," people looking for something, some magic belief or affiliation to fill up their lives.

Lastly, there is an on-going quest for ultimate power. People want control over the now, the future, and especially over lives of other individuals. When Simon the Sorcerer, who by definition was a religious figure, made an offer to purchase the power of the Holy Spirit; the Apostle Peter immediately rebuked the proposal and identified him as a child of the devil (Acts 8:20-25).

Sorcery is the satanic practice of influencing or controlling the lives of people through demonic influence. Unfortunately, many people, including Christians are still involved with Satanism and various types of occult practices to include astrology (zodiac signs/charts), secret societies, séances, Wicca practices, satanic music, Spiritism (chanting, channeling and conjuring) and mystic forms of dark magic.

The Bible warns us to avoid these evil practices:

> "When you enter the land the Lord your God is giving you, do not learn to imitate the detestable ways of the nations there. Let no one be found among you who sacrifices their son or daughter in the fire, who practices divination or sorcery, interprets omens, engages in witchcraft, or casts spells, or who is a medium or spiritist or who consults the dead. Anyone who does these things is detestable to the Lord; because of these same detestable practices the Lord your God will drive out those nations before you. You must be blameless before the Lord your God" (Deuteronomy 18:9-13 NIV).

[1] Willa Appel, *Cults in America, Programmed for Paradise* (Holt, Rinehart and Winston, 1983), p.59

ORIGINS OF EVIL (scriptural text support)

In the beginning Satan was an archangel under God's service. But one day he revolted against God and got a third of the angels with him. After the rebellion, Satan was casted down from heaven along with the other revolting angels. Since then, Satan and his hordes of fallen angels (that are now called demons and evil spirits) have done their best to corrupt, kill and destroy every living soul but he especially despises we who are practitioners of Jesus' teachings.

SATANISM AND THE OCCULT

Satan is envious of God and persistently endeavors to redirect people away from everything associated with God's son, Jesus Christ. Most of all he desires people to worship him, not God. Satanism and the occult are two means of recruiting people away from God. People involved in Satanism and different kinds of occult often believe that merely exploring spirituality, but in reality they are initiating contact with dark and evil forces. Many foolishly labor under the misconception that through sorcery, spells, rituals, séances and mystic games dark forces can be manipulated and controlled, but they are all deceived. No, the occult is not an exercise in the exploration of spirituality! This is not a game. The occult is the gateway into bondage and an entrance into hell!

Thinker's NOTES

_____
_____
_____
_____
_____
_____
_____
_____
_____
_____
_____
_____
_____
_____
_____
_____
_____
_____
_____
_____
_____
_____
_____

Thinker's NOTES

JESUS – The Deliverer

When Jesus died on the cross and rose on the third day, He conquered Satan and all his demons. (Colossians 2:15, Hebrews 2:14) Christians must never be afraid of Satan! Lucifer is defeated. The Lord Jesus Christ is the real source of delivering power (1 John 4:4, Matthew 28:18). Through Jesus' victory on the cross, we are more than conquerors capable of breaking all strongholds through the power of the Holy Spirit, prayer, discipline and the application of Jesus' name. Remember all demonic power is subject to the name that is above all names (Philippians 2:9-10).

A closer examination of this encounter in Acts 13 reveals precisely what occult practitioners, knowingly or unknowingly, truly are:

1. They are in a league with Satan and possess certain supernatural powers.

2. They are false prophets.

3. They seek to influence people politically and ecclesiastically, particularly those in positions of authority (v. 6-7).

4. They attempt to prevent those who are seeking to hear the Word of God from learning it by opposing those who preach it (v. 8).

5. They deliberately attempt to divert prospective converts from the faith as their ultimate goal (v. 8).

In contrast to this, the judgment of the Holy Spirit is explicit:

1. He calls such attempts and practices "full of all kinds of deceit and trickery" (v. 10 NIV).

2. He designates occultism and the occult as having its origin with the devil, by calling Bar-jesus "son of the devil" (v. 10).

3. He unmasks the occultists' tactics and declares them to be enemies of all that is righteous. He calls them perverters of the ways of the Lord, which are designated as "straight," or right (v. 10).

Thinker's NOTES

_____

_____

_____

_____

_____

_____

_____

Generation REVOLT – In Search of Truth

The escalation of occult participation among America's youth (18-30) is a direct result of an apathetic church. Of course, there are other factors such as: (1) the failure of organized religion to meet the needs of a rapidly changing American demographic; (2) unprepared (lack of training, experience, and vision) pastoral leaders; and lastly, rigid congregational cultural traditions.

There is a spiritual revolt against churches and Christian educational institutions, e.g., seminaries incorporating Christological teachings involving science and technology. People, especially youth, are tired of testing and validating truth by the empirical method. In other words, in their spiritual revolt against Christ's church, they are looking for something outside of historical Jesus. People want to know that the Jesus of our Bible is real! Young people are demanding to know that the power of the "Day of Pentecost" was real and still exist!

Moreover, there is a rebellion against materialism. In an affluent and materialistic society, young people turn to drugs, alcohol, and illicit sex to escape reality. GenXers and Millennials rebel in multiple ways because they reject a society that displays little concern or intolerance for so many. Instead, they pursue a new reality to fill the vacuum of the soul, and Satan stands ready to supply that reality with pseudo satisfaction.

Furthermore, there is a rejection of religion in general. Many people believe it is responsible for the world's problems, and they turn away from Christianity in particular because the Church is in an age of apostasy. It is in a state of corruption, rejecting the sacred truths of righteousness yet preserving the outward appearances—the form—of godliness, without the power intrinsic within the faith (2 Tim. 3:5).

Lastly, believe it or not many of the attacks that occur against Christianity in the midst of this revolt do not come from liberal philosophers or agnostic scientists; the most devastating attacks originate from callous religious scoffers sitting on pews, standing in pulpits and lecturing in schools of divinity or theological seminaries.

The slings and arrows against the faith come from those who should be out preaching the gospel and defending the faith; the shepherds set to watch the sheep. It is an ominous but irrefutable fact that the worst enemies of the faith are often those commissioned to proclaim it.

Thinker's NOTE

_____

_____

_____

_____

_____

_____

SECTION TWO
The Occult Revolution

Pride Precedes Destruction (Proverbs 16:18-19)

- Occultist define the occult as truth; a deeper, more profound truth than the Bible can prove or the verifiable facts provided by science

- Occultism is built upon the "Knowledge of experience"

- Experience is not subject to divine authority – nor is it in any capacity relevant

- Death is not a violent result of sin, it has no sting, and it is neither friend or enemy

In Romans 1:18–32, the apostle Paul details the deviation of man's worship from God-inspired to a demonically inspired, polytheistic worship of beasts, fowl, and insects. He informs us that mankind's spiritual descent into false religions worldwide resulted from suppressing God's "truth in unrighteousness" (v. 18). The key element in Romans is that God "gave them up to uncleanness" (v. 24), which was followed by their creature worship. This "uncleanness" is a vast, all-inclusive area that embraces such base practices as animism, Paganism, and varied occult rituals.

In discussing prehistoric occult activities among ancient civilizations, Old Testament scholar Merrill Unger notes that "traffic in the realm of evil spirits goes back in most ancient times to the antediluvian world . . . The earliest history of Egypt, Mesopotamia, and the Graeco-Roman world is replete with examples of cultivation of the demoniacal arts." In Paul's continued theme, fallen man was carried away through "the lusts of their hearts, to dishonor their bodies among themselves" (Rom. 1:24). At first glance, this indicates sexual perversion, but it is important to note the plural "lusts," which does not limit the lusts to sexuality and could represent all forms of dishonoring the body. These "lusts" were often found in occult rituals and the ancient Paganism that embraced it, sexual perversion being central to many Pagan rites, which harmonizes with the "vile passions" found in verse 26. Paul's conclusion is that man, left to his own devices, never ascends to God on his own, but descends into the basest religious forms, including secret and hidden practices that are passed from one initiation to another.

David Moore, a writer for the Gallup Organization, analyzes the American interest in the occult: "A recent Gallup survey shows that just about three in four Americans hold some paranormal belief—in at least one of the following: extra sensory perception (ESP), haunted houses, ghosts, mental telepathy, clairvoyance, astrology, communicating with the dead, Witches, reincarnation, and channeling." According to Gallup, this 2005 poll shows "little change" from the original poll four years earlier (2001). With the population of the United States hovering around 300 million people, these believers would account for approximately 225 million Americans. In view of these statistics, the number of adherents worldwide must be astronomical. This does not indicate that those who believe in it also practice it, but belief is generally the first step toward practice.

14

Occultism: The Art of Seduction

The occult seduces the unwary with its offer of limited knowledge of the future and supposed control over the lives of others. It promises power. If someone involved in the occult can provide secret information to an individual that only he knows, and then predict something that does indeed occur, then the occultist has secured power over the other person through fear of intimidation.

The occult holds out the promise of love, but it is not the divine, unconditional love of God (agape) as described in the sacred Word of God. Rather, it is psychosexual love (eros), which explains why many of those who are in the world of the occult are immoral, recognizing only a standard of authority established by their own reasoning. The occult offers a small degree of certainty in a world of chaotic uncertainty. Moving outside the realm of established religion, it promises things that the Church forbids. It provides a sense of belonging, so desperately needed by people who reject God's love in Jesus Christ, and accept substitutes rather than regeneration in the image of God through faith in Lord Jesus Christ.

At its heart it is egocentric: the occultist seeks first his own ends and then the ends of others. It provides no exit from the realities of life and the problem of sin, but is merely a satanic diversion that frequently masks itself in Christian terminology. That is why we are experiencing a sharp rise in Spiritualism. The Spiritualism Doctrine proposes that we focus on the nature and origin of "spirits," and their relation with the corporeal (physical/tangible) world. There are churches that deny the deity of Jesus Christ, His atonement on the Cross for our sins, and His bodily resurrection, yet still use Christian terminology, quote the Bible, and sing hymns (altered to fit their theological structure).

They have the form of Christianity, as did Simon the sorcerer in Acts. However, they are devoid of the Christocentric gospel model (2 Tim. 3:5). It should come as no surprise to us that Satan created a bogus historical Jesus and an altered gospel model (2 Cor. 11:4). Satan introduced pseudo-Christian practices that seem to model a biblical pattern but culminate in eternal death.

The revolt against reason and logic today has brought on the drug culture and a yearning for some sense of security. It has brought on the increased consumption of alcohol and deadly designer drugs. And now, our nation is plagued with an epidemic of virtual sex in every facet of society including Christendom. This demonic revolt against godliness has produced an immoral humanistic rebellion. The aftermath has created fertile grounds for occultism. In direct opposition to these false satanic doctrines are the good sound doctrines of Holy Scripture. These doctrines were ordained by Christ and taught by the apostles. These sacred doctrines alone are pure and true. They originated from God Himself. God adjures us through the Holy Spirit to continue in the things we have learned from His Word. He implores us to study to show ourselves approved, faithful handlers of the Word of Truth (2 Tim. 2:15).

Thinker's Reflections

Why is there such a tremendous development in the field of occultism? What is the powerful force driving it? The easy answer is "the devil is behind it," but in this case, the easy answer also happens to be the truth: the devil is behind it. The Scripture says he is "the god of this age" and "the prince of the power of the air" (2 Cor. 4:4, Eph. 2:2).

_____
_____
_____
_____
_____
_____
_____
_____
_____
_____
_____
_____
_____
_____
_____
_____
_____
_____
_____
_____
_____
_____
_____
_____
_____
_____
_____
_____
_____
_____
_____
_____

The Doctrine of the Demons

O' How Thou Art Fallen (Isaiah 14:12-14)

> "How art thou fallen from heaven, O Lucifer, son of the morning! How art thou cut down to the ground, which didst weaken the nations! For thou hast said in thine heart, I will ascend into heaven, I will exalt my throne above the stars of God: I will sit also upon the mount of the congregation, in the sides of the north: I will ascend above the heights of the clouds; I will be like the most High. Yet thou shalt be brought down to hell, to the sides of the pit. they that see thee shall narrowly look upon thee, and consider thee, saying, Is this the man that made the earth to tremble, that did shake kingdoms"

- Satanism tenaciously promotes itself as pure religion and as truth

- This treacherous doctrine teaches that Jesus Christ is not God in incarnate. It insists that Jesus was perfect humanity; Christ was merely a conceptual ideal of God's nobility

- Jesus is one of many equally good ways. He is an aspect of the truth; he is a fragment of the life.

- Secret knowledge of the future exists outside of Jehovah God, and should be pursued and explored

- There are supernatural beings other than God, and they can be contacted and controlled

"Satan" is the personal name of the head of the demons. The name "Satan" is actually a Hebrew term (*satan)* meaning primarily to, "obstruct, oppose," (Numbers 22:22). The New Testament also uses the name "Satan," simply taking it over from the Old Testament. Jesus, in his temptation while in the wilderness, speaks to Satan directly saying, "... Get thee hence, Satan: for it is written, Thou shalt worship the Lord thy God, and him only shalt thou serve" (Matthew 4:10). Additionally, Jesus makes personal reference to Satan, "I saw Satan fall like lightning from heaven" (Luke 10:18).

The Word of God uses other names for Satan. He is called "the devil" (Matthew 4:1; 13-39; 25:41; Revelation 12:9; 20:2). The word devil is an English translation of Greek *diabolos*, which actually means "slander." In fact, the English word devil is ultimately derived from this same Greek word, but the phonetic sound of the word changed considerably as the word passed from Greek to Latin to Old English to modern English. Satan is also called, "the serpent," "Beelzebul," "the ruler of this world," "the prince of the power of the air," and the "evil one."

The doctrine of the demons is to portray Jesus as an admired religious figure. Thus, Jesus Christ is not "the" way to salvation; but in fact, Jesus is just one of many ways to obtain God's salvation.

Thinker's NOTES

SECTION TWO
Lucifer & His Three Principal Teachings

"Satan" is the personal name of the head of the demons. The name "Satan" is actually a Hebrew term (*satan)* meaning primarily to, "obstruct, oppose," (Numbers 22:22).

Satan and his demons seek to blind people to the gospel (2 Corinthians 4:4) and keep them in bondage to things that hinder them from coming to God (Galatians 4:8). They will utilize every means at their disposal including, temptation, doubt, guilt, fear, confusion, sickness, envy, pride, and slander to hinder a people from serving and developing a spiritual relationship with God.

Three Principle Teachings of the *Greek daimon* and *daimonion*:

1. 1st Principle Teachings: Portray Jesus as an admired historical religious figure: 1st Principal is to discredit Jesus – challenge His deity (The Discovery Channel)

Thinker's Consideration (Acts 16:14-18)

> 14. And a certain woman named Lydia, a seller of purple, of the city of Thyatira, which worshipped God, heard us: whose heart the Lord opened, that she attended unto the things which were spoken of Paul. 15. And when she was baptized, and her household, she besought us, saying, If ye have judged me to be faithful to the Lord, come into my house, and abide there. And she constrained us. 16. And it came to pass, as we went to prayer, a certain damsel possessed with a spirit of divination met us, which BROUGHT HER MASTERS much gain by soothsaying: 17. The same followed Paul and us, and cried, saying, These men are the servants of the most high God, which shew unto us [the] way of salvation. 18. And this did she many days. But Paul, being grieved, turned and said to the spirit, I command thee in the name of Jesus Christ to come out of her. And he came out the same hour.

2. 2nd Principal Teaching: Jesus Christ is not "the" way to salvation; but in fact, Jesus is just one of many ways to obtain God's salvation. The Apostolic Doctrine of the Teaching of the Apostles emphasizes that Jesus is the ONLY way to complete deliverance: St. John 14:6 Jesus saith unto him, I AM THE WAY, the truth, and the life: no man cometh unto the Father, but by me: Therefore, in order to persuade people to depart from the "FAITH" you must seduce them by introducing popularize concepts of other ways to God. Oprah, Tom Cruise, celebrities, etc.

3. 3rd Principal Teaching: Devalue and discredit the church, i.e., all spirit-filled born again believers.

Satanic Tactics and Objectives

The ultimate goal of demons is to prevent us from receiving salvation through Jesus Christ. However, when that fails, immediately they work at preventing Christian maturity. Evil spirits persist at wearing Christians down and making them ineffective in the faith. The chief objective is to try to get people to turn away from God through many forms of temptation, harassment, and also from challenging the validity of God's Word in the mind of believers.

Demons are masterful liars. They have perfected various forms of treachery, deception and deceitfulness. My great-grandmother often said, "Satan in a lying wonder!" Satan relentlessly works to make people lie to themselves in an effort to justify behavior contradictory to the Word of God. He will convince the masses that human cruelty, intolerance and social injustice is perfectly acceptable. He is the architect of lying and dishonesty. In addition to lying, another demonic tool is manifested in the form of emotional harassment. Emotional harassment is unwarranted accusation and criticism. Demons will repeatedly interject condemning thoughts into the minds of believers.

"Satan's objective is not to steal, kill, or destroy. **This is because these three things are not objectives. Stealing, killing, and destroying are tactics.** Frankly, Satan is perfectly happy to let you live, and prosper, and remain whole and in good health as long as you give him what he wants. What does Satan want? What is his objective as opposed to his tactics? We find Satan's objective in Isaiah 14:13-14. "You said in your heart, 'I will ascend to Heaven; I will raise my throne above the stars of God, and I will sit on the mount of the assembly in the recesses of the north. I will ascend above the heights of the clouds; I will make myself like the Most High. **Satan's objective is to become like God,** to literally replace God on his throne. Not convinced? Look what Satan said to Jesus in Matthew 4:9, "All these things will I give you if you fall down and worship me." Imagine, Satan commanding God to worship him. So, we see that Satan's objective is to become like God. In order to accomplish his objective he has many strategies and tactics. As an example, have you ever wondered why Satan has created so many false religious systems in the world that believe so many different and contradictory things? It's really rather simple. As long as we stay away from Jesus, as long as we ignore his word, we enthrone Satan."

~ Author Tom Terry

As an educator, I assure you that the thing you repeatedly hear, you will eventually believe! Whatever is believed is acted on. Whatever is acted on decides life's outcomes. Demons are on a "seek to destroy your life" mission. Demons strategize. They take advantage of our weaknesses, particularly when we are either physically and/or emotionally weak or vulnerable.

Think on These Things...

There are several ways by which demons oppress people:

- Afflict: to inflict with something unpleasant or harmful
- Devalue: to cause you to feel less than your worth
- Falsely Accuse: to wrongfully defame by lying
- Harass: to annoy or disturb persistently, to wear out by frequent attacks
- Intimidate: to frighten by threatening
- Influence: to exercise indirect power over in order to sway or affect
- Oppress: to lower in spirit or mood
- Torment: to cause severe suffering of body or mind
- Torture: to punish or coerce by inflicting excruciating pain
- Worry: to disturb one or destroy one's peace of mind by repeated or persistent torment
- Wrong: to inflict injury on another without justification

REFLECTIONS

WITCHCRAFT

- *Do not turn to mediums or seek out spiritists, for you will be defiled by them. I am the LORD your God (Leviticus 19:31)*

- I Samuel 15:23. "For rebellion is as the sin of witchcraft (worship of something other than God), and stubbornness (worship of one's self or ideals) is as iniquity and idolatry. Because thou hast rejected the Word of the Lord, He hath also rejected thee from being king."

> **Witch** – one that is credited with usually malignant supernatural powers; especially: a woman practicing usually black witchcraft often with the assistance of a devil or familiar spirit, esp. sorceress (2) a practitioner of Wicca.

> **Witchcraft** – the practice of sorcery or black magic (2) conjuring of familiar spirits to perform feats of healing or entertainment through mediums, priestesses, sorcerers, wizards, magicians, healers, shamans and enchantresses.

We are partakers of sorcery when we purposely work in opposition to God. The Bible warns us to not give place to the devil. Bewitchment, conjuring and wizardry are just a few names for operating in the mode of witchcraft. Willfully surrendering control of your mind, body and spirit to demonic forces is the epitome of witchcraft.

Satan operates through the manipulation of people under his evil influence. For example, if Satan wants one of his disciples in a higher position within a company, he has to have an evil spirit in a person of authority to advance the preferred person. If the devil wants to negatively impact a Christian's reputation, he might use an evil spirit of envy to incite a resentful person to speak slanderous lies. This operation is not exclusive to Christians, it works in all groups.

Witchcraft is a destructively effective weapon in Satan's arsenal. It is meant to destroy or prevent anyone from coming into the full knowledge of God through Christ. Witchcraft is an occult practice. The two activities are interconnected. All occult influenced practices are designed to be beautiful snares. That is precisely what witchcraft does; it beautifully ensnares the soul or anyone participating.

Here is a partial list of snares the devil uses:

God tells us to turn to him and renounce the occult. Many people, including Christians, think it's harmless to look at astrological charts or engage in various forms of spiritism. They think it is fun or entertaining. Others look to astrology, divination, and mediums for literal day-to-day guidance. Astrology is not just entertainment for that segment of the population.

God clearly warns against such practices. Listed below are a few scriptural warnings against engaging in any form of the occult:

- We are opening ourselves up to evil spirits

- We are not looking to God for guidance, but to the occult

- We are turning away from "The faith" – giving heed to seducing spirits (1 Timothy 4:1)

Why is witchcraft such an effective tool for the occult?

- Many of those who believed now came and openly confessed their evil deeds. A number who had practiced sorcery brought their scrolls together and burned them publicly. When they calculated the value of the scrolls, the total came to fifty thousand drachmas. In this way the word of the Lord spread widely and grew in power. (Acts 19:18-20)

_____
_____
_____
_____
_____
_____
_____
_____
_____
_____
_____
_____
_____
_____
_____
_____
_____

Case Studies in Disobedience

The Israelites often made the same mistake and turned from God, although God clearly warned them about the heinous practice of witchcraft.

When you enter the land the LORD your God is giving you, do not learn to imitate the detestable ways of the nations there. Let no one be found among you who sacrifices his son or daughter in the fire, who practices divination or sorcery, interprets omens, engages in witchcraft, or casts spells, or who is a medium or who consults the dead. Anyone who does these things is detestable to the LORD, and because of these detestable practices the LORD your God will drive out those nations before you. You must be blameless before the LORD your God. The nations you will dispossess listen to those who practice sorcery or divination. But as for you, the LORD your God has not permitted you to do so. (Deuteronomy 18:9-14)

Why did the citizens of Israel persist on practicing these sinful rituals? What were the outcomes of the practices?

_____

_____

_____

_____

_____

Saul, Israel's first king, started out well. He expelled mediums and spiritists from the land, then violated God's word and his own conscience by consulting a medium (1 Samuel 28:3-25). His end was tragic and Israel's outcome was catastrophic (1 Samuel 31:1-6). What situation created Saul's intense need to consult a medium?

_____

_____

_____

_____

_____

Bible verses warning about mediums and spiritists

1. *Do not turn to mediums or seek out spiritists, for you will be defiled by them. I am the LORD your God. (Leviticus 19:31)*

2. *I will set my face against the person who turns to mediums and spiritists to prostitute himself by following them, and I will cut him off from his people. (Leviticus 20:6)*

3. *When men tell you to consult mediums and spiritists, who whisper and mutter, should not a people inquire of their God? Why consult the dead on behalf of the living? (Isaiah 8:19)*

Astrology

Astrology – The single most popular realm of the occult is astrology, which deceives countless people through daily horoscopes

Horoscope/Zodiac Readings: The Amusing & Exciting Form of Divination

THINK on These FACTS

- Astrology is the ancient practice of interpreting the stars and the position of the planets to forecast national destiny, personal character, or personal destiny.

- Historically astrologers believed in a direct causal connection between heavenly bodies and earth, but some modern astrologers see the link as more spiritual than causal.

- Astrology usurps God's sovereignty and authority, and it is condemned as an abomination in the Old Testament.

The Word of the Lord declares: "The heavens declare the glory of God; and the firmament shows the work of his hands" (Psalm 19:1). One writer said, "When I consider thy heavens, the work of thy fingers, the moon and the stars, which thou ordained" (Psalm 8:3). The heavens are majestic and gloriously beautiful. I have observed the sun rise in Tokyo, Japan (land of the rising sun). I have marveled at the noon day sun's calmness atop of Gohwangsan Mountains in Seoul, Korea (land of the morning calm). I have watched the moon rise from the white sandy beaches of Ft. Lauderdale, Florida. Yes, I have gazed the stars at night from the astonishingly beautiful Sandia Mountains in Albuquerque, New Mexico. Nothing, however, compares to being captivated by the flaming firmament of a reddish orange sunset from Manhattan Beach, California.

These experiences are equivalent to watching God express His heart-felt emotions on an infinite canvas. His glorious resplendency splashed on the atmosphere in breath-taking colorful design! My great-grandmother expressed it this way, "There's nobody like Him!" Regrettably, the awe-inspiring beauty of His design has caused many to search for spiritual instructions and daily guidance by deriving meaning through celestial formations.

Astrological interpretation considers the influence of stars and planets on human affairs. The notion that any particular celestial format can have an impact on your existence is not only scientifically unfounded, it is biblically errant. There are numerous scriptural references warning and forbidding the children of Israel to worship "host of heaven" (Deuteronomy 4:19). Repeatedly, however, God's people participated in the practice of astrological interpretation (2 Kings 17:16). God's Holy Word identifies astrology as a form of divination (Deuteronomy 18:10-14). All astrologers were to receive God's wrathful judgment (Isaiah 47:13-14).

Natal Astrology and Mundane Astrology

The two most popular branches of predictive astrology are known as natal astrology and mundane astrology. Natal astrology, also called genethliacal astrology, makes a prediction based on a person's character, present situation or future outlook beginning with a birth date (or a date of conception, for a few minor astrologists). Mundane astrology usually makes a prediction on a larger scale for a national, civil, or political leadership future. Ancient astrologers followed diverse methods for predicting, forecasting, and studying the stars, much of which was passed down from generation to generation. Historical evidence traces ancient astrology and the zodiac from Mesopotamia to its neighboring countries. These countries, in turn, synthesized it for their needs and cultural adaptation. People groups that lacked knowledge of the biblical Creator satisfied their religious cravings by viewing planets and stars as gods and then developing their belief system.

Five Respective Goals of Astrological Divination

1. The first goal of astrologers is to penetrate the future. Astrology appeals to so many people because they want to pierce the hidden veil of the future.

2. A second purpose of astrology is the attempt to bring order out of chaos. This aim appeals to the desire for something sensible in a chaotic world.

3. A third objective is the art of character analysis. By interpreting the position of the planets in a zodiacal house at the point of birth and then matching it to past astrological theories, the stars may reveal character and destiny.

4. A fourth goal astrologers hope to achieve is a successful appeal to people's need for purpose and self-empowerment. People want their lives to have meaning; they look for ways to tap into personal power.

5. A fifth and final aim of astrologers is to gain validity by appealing to antiquity or biblical authority. Serious astrologers will firmly maintain that nothing in astrology contradicts the Bible.

Scriptural Reflection

- Do not practice divination or sorcery. (Leviticus 19:26)

- Therefore this is what the Sovereign LORD says: "I am against your magic charms with which you ensnare people like birds and I will tear them from your arms; I will set free the people that you ensnare like birds." (Ezekiel 13:20)

- The idols speak deceit, diviners see visions that lie; they tell dreams that are false, they give comfort in vain. Therefore the people wander like sheep oppressed for lack of a shepherd. (Zechariah 10:2)

- "So I will come near to you for judgment. I will be quick to testify against sorcerers, adulterers and perjurers, against those who defraud laborers of their wages, who oppress the widows and the fatherless, and deprive aliens of justice, but do not fear me," says the LORD Almighty. (Malachi 3:5)

- And when you look up to the sky and see the sun, the moon and the stars—all the heavenly array—do not be enticed into bowing down to them and worshiping things the LORD your God has apportioned to all the nations under heaven. (Deuteronomy 4:19)

- ... and contrary to my command has worshiped other gods, bowing down to them or to the sun or the moon or the stars of the sky. (Deuteronomy 17:3)

- All the counsel you have received has only worn you out! Let your astrologers come forward, those stargazers who make predictions month by month, let them save you from what is coming upon you. Surely they are like stubble; the fire will burn them up. They cannot even save themselves from the power of the flame. Here are no coals to warm anyone; here is no fire to sit by. That is all they can do for you—these you have labored with and trafficked with since childhood. Each of them goes on in his error; there is not one that can save you. (Isaiah 47:13-15)

- Hear what the LORD says to you, O house of Israel. This is what the LORD says: "Do not learn the ways of the nations or be terrified by signs in the sky, though the nations are terrified by them." (Jeremiah 10:1-2)

- In every matter of wisdom and understanding about which the king questioned them, he found them ten times better than all the magicians and enchanters in his whole kingdom. (Daniel 1:20)

REFLECTIONS

What is your opinion of believers relying on the horoscopes?

You shall not make for yourself an idol in the form of anything in heaven above or on the earth beneath or in the waters below. You shall not bow down to them or worship them; for I, the LORD your God, am a jealous God, punishing the children for the sin of the fathers to the third and fourth generation of those who hate me. (Exodus 20:4-5)

Watch yourselves very carefully, so that you do not become corrupt and make for yourselves an idol, an image of any shape, whether formed like a man or a woman, or like any animal on earth or any bird that flies in the air, or like any creature that moves along the ground or any fish in the waters below. (Deuteronomy 4:15-18)

_____
_____
_____
_____
_____
_____
_____
_____
_____
_____
_____
_____
_____
_____
_____
_____
_____
_____
_____
_____
_____
_____
_____
_____
_____
_____
_____
_____

Psychic Phenomena

THINK on These FACTS

- Psychic or paranormal phenomena (its modern label) are genuine experiences that cannot be explained by scientific observation; they are experiences of the body, soul and spirit that appeal to the inquisitive nature of man.

- These phenomena include Extrasensory Perception (ESP) and Psychokinesis (PK)

- There are two forms of the phenomenon called ESP: normal and occult

- Satan is the power behind occult psychic phenomena; its purpose is to deceive mankind and lead people away from God

- Hypnotism is not a psychic phenomenon, but it can be used in conjunction with occult tools such as regression therapy and automatic writing

- Biblical texts, taken out of context, are often used to justify psychic events

The purpose of all occult psychic phenomena, both ancient (Nostradamus) and modern (Jean Dixon), is deception. These phenomena, manifested long ago by the magicians of Egypt who imitated the miracles of God, are meant to duplicate and destroy—as the Antichrist will duplicate the miracles of Jesus in order to deceive and destroy humanity (Rev. 13:15). They do not lead people toward God, but away from Him.

Psychic phenomena intrigue many people because they involve the strange and the extraordinary, offering secrecy, excitement, and power to a world that loves anything cloaked in mystery.

What exactly are psychic phenomena? Psychic simply comes from the Greek word psuke, which refers to the soul. Phenomena refers to experiences: the things that people see, hear, smell, taste, touch, or comprehend. Psychic phenomena (also called Psi by interested scholars) are events that cannot be explained by scientific observation. They are experiences of the soul; things that appeal to the spiritual nature of man.

Parapsychology is the study of psychic phenomena including extrasensory perception (ESP) and psychokinesis (PK). Para in the Greek means "alongside," and psychology means the study of the psyche or the soul or the spiritual facility sometimes known as the mind. Extrasensory perception is a term coined by ESP researcher Dr. J. B. Rhine and defined in Man, Myth, and Magic as "the reception of information by a person through other means than the senses." It is data received through means other than the customary channels of information.

Occult ESP can be divided into three main categories for the purpose of definition: clairvoyance, precognition, and medium trance. Clairvoyance, also called remote viewing, is the capacity to access knowledge from a source not related to the human mind; this source is always demonic. The information can be linked to an object and/or event located far from the actual physical presence of the person. Precognition is knowledge of events that have not yet taken place. These projected events may be days, weeks, or months in the future—sometimes even years. The information has nothing to do with human-to-human contact, and everything to do with human-to-demon contact.

A medium trance is a direct physical encounter with demonic personalities, usually triggered by attempts to speak to the dead. Demons imitate the bodies and voices of the departed, but Scripture says a great gulf is fixed between the living and the dead (Luke 16:26). No one is permitted to cross this gulf—so who is impersonating lost loved ones? The Bible warns of the power of demonic beings, ancient enemies who use whatever tools they have at their disposal to deceive people—imitating the voices and faces of beloved relatives, and parroting back their words—all for the purpose of luring grieving families and curious spectators ever closer to demonic influence and control.

The purpose of psychic phenomena is to deceive. Psychics are expert illusionist. Practitioners of psychic phenomena are imitators of spiritual reality. They deceive followers by convincing them that death can be conquered through human powers.

Belief in psychic phenomena is a substitute for faith in the God of the Bible and in His Son, Jesus Christ. These phenomena can only imitate what faith in God through Christ promises: the conquest of fear and death, and power for living here on this earth. What the Christian obtains as a gift from God through the power of the Holy Spirit, people dabbling in the occult obtain by satanic means. God is not in the least bit interested in participating in occult psychic phenomena.

The Word of God teaches that at the end of the ages, the Church should anticipate the outgrowth of great spiritual darkness. This is a work of the devil, and if Christians remain silent in the middle of an entire generation given over to the pursuit of occult Psi phenomena—a generation making a concerted attempt to take over the Word of God and use its terms to describe satanic phenomena—then today's Christians will bequeath chaos to the Church of tomorrow. A clear delineation must be made; someone must say, "Here is God and there is Satan."

The Lord Jesus Christ walked on the water, He did not levitate on it! Philip was not teleported, and there is no such thing as apportation in biblical theology. Philip was moved by the Spirit of God from one place to the other, which is much different from moving an ashtray from one room to another or appearing and disappearing in a railway station. And finally, the Word of God indicates that when it comes to the interpretation of dreams, God has a corner on the market. If someone wants to know what a dream means, then he or she should pray about it. In fact, we should pray about anything disturbing, because without prayer, it will continue to disturb, even if the disturbance is occurring during unconsciousness.

It is not necessary to see a psychiatrist or a psychologist or to read "Dream Analysis for Dummies" to find out the meaning of dreams. Genesis 40:8 says, "Do not interpretations [of dreams] belong to God?" The answer is yes, they do. God holds the key to all interpretation. The word interpret in Hebrew is pathar, which means "to open up."[53] Do not inquire of the wizards or the mediums; ask the Lord for direct information. "And when they say to you 'Seek those who are mediums and wizards, who whisper and mutter,' should not a people seek their God? Should they seek the dead on behalf of the living?" (Isa. 8:19–20). God is the one who will provide information, and He is willing (up to a point) to give people that assurance.

The purpose of occult psychic phenomena is to imitate. The purpose of imitation is deception—to lead us away from the Lord our God (Deut. 13:5). Why are people attracted to this type of paranormal activity?

- It is the unknown—and exciting.

- It is mystifying and appeals to the carnal nature.

- It is a display of power outside of man's capacity to control it.

- It is a substitute for the voice of God.

- It is a spiritual narcotic.

A pharmaceutical narcotic affects the brain and the central nervous system, producing a feeling of well-being. It creates hallucinations and generally tends to remove the subject from reality. This change is the product of a chemical narcotic phenomenon, and the same effect is precisely what occurs in the realm of the spirit. The moment an individual accepts occult phenomena and believes them implicitly, the phenomena become a substitute for reality in the dimension of the spirit. The psychic dimension of the occult is a narcotic that anesthetizes man's spiritual nature and makes him insensitive to the reality of God so he does not hear the voice of God—he hears other voices.

NOTES

_____
_____
_____
_____
_____
_____
_____
_____
_____
_____
_____
_____

REFLECTIONS

What have you observed in mass media today that promotes ESP and PK?

What psychic phenomena have you seen in society?

Why do you think people seek psychic phenomenal experiences?

_____
_____
_____
_____
_____
_____
_____
_____
_____
_____
_____
_____
_____
_____
_____
_____
_____
_____
_____
_____
_____
_____
_____
_____
_____
_____
_____
_____
_____

REFLECTIONS

What is your opinion on churches that use information provided by psychics?

_____
_____
_____
_____
_____
_____
_____
_____
_____
_____
_____
_____
_____
_____
_____
_____
_____
_____
_____
_____
_____
_____
_____
_____
_____
_____
_____
_____
_____
_____
_____

Traditional Religions

World Religions – an organized system of beliefs, ceremonies, and rules used to worship a god or group of gods: an interest, a belief, or an activity that is very important to a person

Major World Religions – Christianity, Hinduism, Judaism, Islam, Buddhism & (New Age)

THINK on These FACTS

- The belief in a Supreme Being is central to traditional religions; lesser deities exist, but they serve the Supreme Being

- Powerful forces exist in the universe, and these forces can be consulted and utilized to accomplish good or evil

- Religion and mystical connectivity are inseparable; magic has the power to influence the gods and spirits

- Jesus is not the *only* way to God

- There is no devil and no original sin

REFLECTIONS

What is your perspective on the major world religions?

_____

_____

_____

_____

_____

_____

_____

_____

_____

_____

_____

_____

_____

_____

_____

_____

_____

_____

_____

_____

_____

_____

_____

_____

_____

_____

_____

_____

_____

_____

_____

_____

_____

SECTION THREE
Demon Possession and Exorcism

THINK on These FACTS

- Satan is the power behind all occult psychic phenomena; his purpose is to deceive mankind and lead people away from God.

- Demon possession is a common occurrence, not a rare phenomenon.

- Jesus taught exorcism by example, and the Church must follow His lead.

- One should never enter into battle against the world of the occult without prayer.

SATAN SEEKS TO CONTROL YOUR MIND

Mind control is the most lethal weapon in Satan's arsenal. He uses it to control the born again believer. The Scriptures admonish us to "bring every thought into captivity", II Corinthians 10:5. The Scriptures say that the spirit of a sound mind means a disciplined mind. It is absolutely essential for a person to keep a sound mind or a disciplined mind, to become aware of the thoughts that are coming from the devil and the thoughts that are coming from the Lord. Many times a person will enter a world of fantasy and imagination, lusting after something, or covetousness, or of something they consider normal. Many times they will dwell on what to do in case of an accident. This is a great counterfeit when the devil will have you go over and over what to do in case of an accident. By accepting this and hearing this in our mind we are giving place to the devil for it to happen.

This is a counterfeit for what we are supposed to do when these thoughts enter our minds. We should reject them and reassure ourselves that it cannot happen to us because the protection is available that the Lord has promised in His scriptures. Psalm 91 and other great scriptures should enter our mind and we should control the thoughts and possess total victory over those situations. We should dispose or cast out these thoughts of the devil and not entertain them.

It's important to "capture our thoughts." By apprehending our thoughts, understanding our thoughts, and being able to look upon our own thoughts, we can bring every thought into captivity. Many times a split personality could stop the personality from changing by simply taking charge of his own thoughts. It is important to realize that things like Dungeons and Dragons, and other games of witchcraft, put the mind in gear for Satan. Then witchcraft activity becomes common place. The casting of spells, the inducing of charms, and the practicing of witchcraft takes over the entire mind and thus gives way to the mind control spirit whereby the mind can be controlled by the devil himself. This is also the reason for the psychedelic colors in the Rubik's cube, and the mind boggling disco lights and the lights that are sold as rhythm, colors. All these colors affect the mentality and aid in the taking over and controlling of the mind.

The prime root cause for failure to use spiritual gifts is Mind Control. Beelzebub interferes with the correct operation of spiritual gifts. Beelzebub desires to skew God's glory. We should ask the Lord to loose spirits of Joshua and Caleb and to help us to take full control, power and authority over Mind Control. The Occult serves as a doorway for darkness. It provides demonic powers that were once removed from your life an opportunity to re-enter. Seal off this entrance with the Blood of Jesus.

REFLECTIONS

The Jesus of the Occult

THINK on These FACTS

- People involved in the occult deny the true history and person of Jesus Christ; He is generally added to occult practices for credibility.

- The "Christ" of the occult is not a unique being; He is not the only Christ.

- Jesus is a great man who discovered principles that can be imitated.

- The name of Jesus may be invoked in some occult practices for added power or authority.

God has identified the Bible as the standard for measuring truth; it reveals everything essential about the person, nature, and work of His Son, Jesus Christ. Yet in spite of biblical warnings forbidding any alteration or manipulation of God's Word, invariably there are those who cross the line and create a false image of Jesus.1 This redefinition of Jesus Christ, crafted to suit personal ends, is nothing more than a repackaging of the same complex lies created and circulated by the Gnostics during the time of the early Church. Throughout his lifetime, the apostle John watched false teachings about Jesus infiltrate the Church, and he responded strongly to the Gnostic heresy by offering proof of his eyewitness testimony to the true person of Jesus Christ:

That which was from the beginning, which we have heard, which we have seen with our eyes, which we have looked upon, and our hands have handled, concerning the Word of life—the life was manifested, and we have seen, and bear witness, and declare to you that eternal life which was with the Father and was manifested to us. (1 John 1:1–2)

Paul's epistle to the Colossians and the epistle of 1 John are recognized by biblical scholars as direct apologetic thrusts against the teachings that spawned this cult: spiritualizing (by metaphor) the Old Testament, redefining contemporary Christian terminology, substituting an impersonal god for the God of revelation, and reducing Jesus Christ to a demigod or a pantheistic emanation from the unknowable divine essence.

The Identity of Jesus taught His disciples that deceivers are relentless in their efforts to alter His identity, so He asked them, "Who do men say that I, the Son of Man, am?" The disciples' answer reveals how unregenerate men desperately tried to explain Jesus Christ: "Some say John the Baptist, some Elijah, and others Jeremiah or one of the prophets." Jesus then asked His disciples for their understanding: "Who do you say that I am?" Peter's answer glowed with revelation: "You are the Christ, the Son of the living God" (Matt. 16:13–16). The unsatisfied curiosity of mankind's soul, in its lost condition, demands an explanation of Jesus. Even those who had access to Christ's earthly ministry falsely concluded that he was John the Baptist, Elijah, Jeremiah, or one of the prophets.

For cultists and occultists, however, connecting Jesus' name to their beliefs and practices gives the illusion of credibility, since so many people have heard of Him. But when Scripture tests their Jesus, he falls miserably short of God's truth; he is never truly their central figure, and he is not core to their beliefs. Jesus is incidental—remaining on the fringe—and inserted wherever they find Him beneficial or acceptable. Their system of self-exaltation exists without Him. Nonbelievers often treat Jesus as a myth or a mystical figure, and their view of the historical Jesus influences their spiritual direction. There are those who deny the trustworthiness of New Testament history and approach Him as a myth in the same way they would approach Krishna, Thor, or Neptune. To them, the name Jesus has nothing to do with a personal Savior. Instead, Jesus is a means to an end: cosmic personal power needed to accomplish a task. By relegating Jesus to myth, they can rewrite and reinvent His life to fit comfortably within their worldview.

Christianity has a long history of distinguishing between fables or myths and historically verifiable truth.

Some occult writers accept Jesus' historical existence yet treat Him as a mystical figure, a man who learned how to use the latent powers that they desire. By transforming Jesus into a Jewish mystic, they change His character, arbitrarily adding false attributes that fit their purpose. The fluidity of mysticism allows them to form Jesus in their personal image as opposed to conforming to His biblical image.

Documentary: The Historical Jesus

Review the Historical Jesus

REFLECTIONS

What is your opinion on the historical Jesus narrative?

_____

_____

_____

_____

_____

_____

_____

_____

_____

_____

_____

_____

_____

_____

_____

_____

_____

_____

_____

_____

_____

_____

_____

_____

_____

_____

_____

_____

_____

_____

_____

_____

_____

_____

_____

Spiritual Warfare

THINK on These FACTS

- The supernatural realm of the occult is centered upon Satan's kingdom, and its power is directly dispensed through him and his demonic servants to the limits of his domain.

- The human realm of the occult is centered upon mankind's sinful nature, which seeks power over self, other beings and circumstances.

- Christians face two spiritual war fronts: one is directly against the powers of Satan, and the other is against the power of sin.

- God has provided authority, power, and victory for Christians over Satan and Satan's representatives, whether demonic or human.

Jesus taught that His followers must be "born from above," commonly translated as "born again" in order to see the kingdom of God (John 3:3). When a person enters the kingdom of God, the prince of darkness incurs an immediate loss, and he then makes it his goal to trouble the new Christian at every opportunity. This engagement of Satan, his power, his works, or his demons is called spiritual warfare. Two conflicting elements define this warfare in individual Christian living: one consists of the wonderful benefits of the abundant life promised by Jesus in John 10:10, replete with miracles, healings, power, signs, wonders, and seemingly unlimited blessings and joy; the other element brings tribulation, trials, temptations, hardships, frustrations, afflictions, illnesses, and spiritual war. Most Christians experience both sides of this conflict, though some endure more of one than the other. The how and why of this division in individual lives is best left to the wisdom of God, whose power it is to change all circumstances.

On the upside of life's difficulties, we also know that God will not allow more trouble or temptation than what we can endure. "No temptation has overtaken you except such as is common to man; but God is faithful, who will not allow you to be tempted beyond what you are able, but with the temptation will also make the way of escape, that you may be able to bear it" (1 Cor. 10:13). The way of escape spoken of here is only a glimpse of the power available to Christians in spiritual warfare, but the sad truth is that this power is not exercised enough to the glory of God in our individual lives. Too often, people become absorbed in self-pity and forget to call upon the Holy Spirit—the Comforter. Many have not been taught to properly exercise their faith in times of need, and Satan delights in weak Christians who have not schooled themselves in the powerful Word of God—a sword intended for daily use by Christians. "For the word of God is living and powerful, and sharper than any two-edged sword, piercing even to the division of soul and spirit, and of joints and marrow, and is a discerner of the thoughts and intents of the heart" (Heb. 4:12) Jesus used the power of God's written Word to defeat Satan's temptations during His time of trial in the wilderness (Luke 4:1–13).

This is one of many examples found in the New Testament that reveal exactly how the Christian can emerge victorious in spiritual warfare. The glorious end of this story is that Jesus defeated Satan's wilderness trials.

"Now when the devil had ended every temptation, he departed from Him until an opportune time" (Luke 4:13). Satan will flee when confronted by the power of God's Word, but it is only to await another opportunity for attack. This is a point Christians would do well to remember, because it demonstrates the strategy of the enemy: Satan may withdraw for a time, but he always returns. This is why the apostle Peter warned the body of Christ that our enemy stalks about "like a roaring lion, seeking whom he may devour" (1 Peter 5:8). We dare not soften our view of a prowling enemy. He is always seeking whom he may devour. He is always accusing the brethren, both day and night (Rev. 12:10). He is no friend of Christ, no friend of Christians, and no friend of the Church of the living God!

We, the Children of the Most High God, battle not one, but a host of enemies in the invisible world, who sometimes manifest themselves or their works in the visible world, and they all delight in seeing Christians distressed and defeated. The Church is not subject to their bidding, since the power of God is greater than all of the works of darkness, but they are an enemy to be reckoned with. The apostle John offered this great encouragement in the fight: "You are of God, little children, and have overcome them, because He who is in you is greater than he who is in the world" (1 John 4:4).

Spiritual warfare on earth began in the Garden of Eden. Satan, who appeared to Eve as a serpent, presented the first temptation to her and, according to the apostle Paul, deceived Eve in her mind: "But I fear, lest somehow, as the serpent deceived Eve by his craftiness, so your minds may be corrupted from the simplicity that is in Christ" (2 Cor. 11:3). The weapon in this first spiritual battle was Satan's intellect. Though once full of wisdom, he chose to envy God and exchanged his wisdom for lies. Jesus said, "He was a murderer from the beginning, and does not stand in the truth, because there is no truth in him. When he speaks a lie, he speaks from his own resources, for he is a liar and the father of it" (John 8:44). Satan's carefully crafted lies caused the first human beings on earth to lose their standing with God. Spiritual warfare commenced at this separation of the first humans, Adam and Eve, from their Creator.

It is because of this knowledge of the true nature of God that demons do everything within their power to lead mankind into the false doctrines that often embrace many gods (polytheism).

The doctrine of demons consists of any doctrine, dogma, creed, canon or policy that opposes God's truth. The Apostle Paul warned his son in the gospel of two demonic mechanisms: seducing/deceiving spirits, and the initiation of false doctrines among men. These evil dynamics open the door for spiritual deception and subsequent bondage.

> "Now the Spirit expressly says that in latter times some will depart from the faith, giving heed to seducing [deceiving] spirits and doctrines of demons."
>
> ~ Paul (1 Timothy 4:1)

43

Spiritual warfare is a fact of Christian living, but unfortunately, some Christians do their utmost to ignore it, thinking it will have no effect upon them. Adverse conditions are usually treated as a common occurrence or brushed off indifferently and treated as anything other than a demonic attack. But spiritual conflict is one method God uses to catch our attention: it is real, and Christians must properly deal with it.

The Word of God warns us about the reality of spiritual war. We are in conflict against the principalities of this world, in conflict against our carnal natures, and most importantly, in conflict against the devil. We will live and die in the narrative of conflict, unless Jesus Christ returns in our lifetime.

Again, the Word of God declares: "For the weapons of our warfare are not carnal but mighty in God for pulling down strongholds, casting down arguments and every high thing that exalts itself against the knowledge of God, bringing every thought into captivity to the obedience of Christ" (2 Cor. 10:4–5). Notice that it is the weapons of *our* warfare— indeed, it is *our* warfare—it is a *personal* war. These weapons have divine power to tear down strongholds, to demolish arguments, and to literally decimate every proud thought that exalts itself against the throne of God, to bring every thought into captivity to the Lord Jesus Christ.

The spiritual war against Christianity is on-going here and now! The battle doesn't dissipate or subside simply by ignoring it. This is the fact of spiritual warfare. We, the born again believers, are not at spiritual war with other human beings. We are at war with the rulers of darkness of this age that manipulate people as pawns on a great chessboard. Yes, we are at war with evil forces arrayed against the Living God. In 1 Timothy 1:18, Paul wrote, "This charge I commit to you, son Timothy, according to the prophecies previously made concerning you, that by them you may wage the good warfare." Another way of translating this last phrase is "war the warfare." Paul used the strongest word imaginable, stratigiki, which is the Greek transliteration for "strategy." Strategy encompasses logistics of combat, polemics, and the necessary tactics of warfare. On this, William D. Mounce wrote, "The terminology is military, describing a soldier at war." It is an inescapable fact that the Christian is committed to spiritual warfare.

REFLECTIONS: Christianity Weaponry (The Armor of God) Ephesians 6:10-18

_____
_____
_____
_____
_____
_____
_____
_____
_____
_____
_____
_____
_____

REFLECTIONS

SECTION FOUR
Christian Counseling and the Occult

- Christians *cannot* be possessed by any type of demon, but they can be harassed and oppressed.

- Non-Christians involved in the occult become vulnerable to demonic oppression and possession.

- The name of Jesus and the power of His Holy Spirit are the only authority on earth the demons fear and obey; Jesus can deliver all people from possession or oppression.

Deliverance MINISTRIES

_____
_____
_____
_____
_____
_____
_____
_____
_____
_____
_____
_____
_____
_____
_____
_____

1. Christian counseling directly related to the occult is a perilous task, and as such it should never be undertaken by anyone without the following qualifications:

2. A personal relationship with Jesus Christ (John 15)

3. Spiritual maturity as evidenced by a consistent display of the fruits of the Spirit in his or her life; a serious commitment to reading the Scripture and prayer; regular attendance and fellowship at a doctrinally sound, Christian church (Gal. 5:16–22; Heb. 10:25)

4. Acknowledgment of the power of the Holy Spirit (1 Cor. 2:14)

5. A calling to serve (John 17:18)

6. Knowledge, training, and experience in the biblical method, analysis, and resolution of occult phenomena (2 Peter 1:5; Col. 1:10; 2 Tim. 2:15)

REFLECTIONS

Evangelism: Reaching the Hearts of People

THINK on These FACTS

- Evangelism in the true biblical sense of the term means a return to the content of the gospel and to the *methods* of the New Testament church—a fiercely personal, door-to-door and neighbor-to-neighbor effort.

- Evangelism and apologetics work hand-in-hand to accomplish the same goal: the salvation of souls.

- Evangelism is an amalgamation of persistent methods in an effort to reach as many people as possible.

Servant Leadership & Evangelism

In this day and age, pastoral leadership, particularly in the area of urban ministries, must include both a profound respect for and a real understanding of the extraordinary and growing range of cultures and backgrounds that increasingly becoming a part of our diversified congregations.

For those of us who are third – or even fourth generation Christians, we were taught to respect everyone in our church and local community, especially those who were senior in age. After all, my great grandparents were former slaves and sharecroppers; they had an uncommonly communal perspective on sharing living-space with those who had "ideologically differences."

During my early years, I was taught that learning how to live with others was not only Christ-like, it was essential for the survival of our family, community, and all humanity. For years, I believed that most Christians had an almost instinctive understanding of the importance of this simple principle: God loves diversity.

I was, however, very wrong. In fact, some of the worst cases of intolerance and prejudice have been committed by people claiming to be God-fearing Christian men and women. Perhaps, the most racially divided hour in the United States of America is 11:00 A.M., on Sunday morning.

As Christians, we may not like to admit it, but the fact is, many born again believers still have challenges worshipping with people whose cultural, ethnic, and racial composite is different from their own. And occasionally, it's not culture, ethnicity, or race – it's just, well, you know, they're weird. There, I said it. We have issues with those who don't resemble the sanctified majority because after all, they're not our congregants and their not normal, right? Right!

During the 80's I had the distinct privilege of living in America's multicultural "Mecca," Los Angeles. Recently, I had the privilege of visiting Bishop Noel Jones and City of Refuge Ministries (COR) in Los Angeles, California. I was pleased by the diversity throughout the assembly, especially among the youth, but most notably among musicians. Toward the rear of the sanctuary several young men wearing sunglasses (some clothed in "red" others in "blue") sat enjoying the presence and Word of the living God. As I sat there in service observing the potpourri of diversity, I thought about how difficult it was during the 80's for many Southern Californians residing in predominantly Black communities to adjust to the influx of Mexican immigrants moving into their "living-space." Now, they were not only sharing the same housing developments, they were sitting next to each other listening to the same gospel message on the same pew in the same church.

When I questioned Bishop Jones about this marvelous model, he replied, "The church has embraced post modernity."

I interpreted his statement literally and figuratively. From the literal perspective, barring an unnecessarily lengthy discussion about apologetics, *post-modernism* seeks to blend Christian faith and referential presuppositions of Scripture, and harmonize these truths with the church existing in the era of modernization. Figuratively, however, I felt Bishop Jones was saying COR, as an anointed body of believers, have decided to lay aside petty divisive differences for the betterment of the greater community-at-large and ultimately, the Kingdom of God. In other words, it was time for a "Contemporary Perspective."

When you consider the history of the church, corrective adjustments were often required in order to fulfill the great commission, "Go ye therefore, and teach all nations, baptizing them in the name of the Father, and of the Son, and of the Holy Ghost: Teaching them to observe all things whatsoever I have commanded you: and, lo, I am with you always, even unto the end of the world. Amen" (Matthew 28:19-20 KJV).

During the Church's apostolic infancy, the Holy Spirit commissioned the Apostle Paul to correct misperceptions about Gentile nations having a right to access salvation 50 AD. From 100- 300 AD, God used men such as Justin Martyr, Irenaeus, Tertullian, Origen, and many others to correct the fallacies about doctrine, especially sanctification, and to rebuff the egregious mistreatment of woman in ministry. It is irrefutable that God used Bonaventure, Thomas Aquinas and Martin Luther to drive reform in the Christian practices and usher in the era of correction known as "The Reformation." God seemingly used this period to instill profundity, perspicuity, hermeneutical and exegetical excellence in the hearts of Christians. One such Christian was John Calvin (1509-1564). Calvin, a masterful linguist of Latin and French, also had knowledge of the languages of the Bible. He knew both Greek and Hebrew. He has been called an "exegetical genius of the first order." His commentaries are still considered invaluable. God greatly used this man's magnificent mind to provide insight to the truths of His Word. Although these great Christian men were mightily used by God, the Church still required more corrective measures.

Three centuries later, in 1901, God would provide yet another miraculous and *revelatory correction.* This time His Spirit moved in the United States at a Bethel Bible College located in Topeka, Kansas. Agnes N. Ozman became the first person in the 19th century to receive the Holy Ghost. This *divine correction* dispelled centuries of erroneous teachings that the Holy Ghost was no longer being "poured out" as in the early days of the church. Interestingly, Bethel College was founded by Charles Fox Parham. Parham was a devout follower of Jesus, like his spiritual ancestral father, the Apostle Peter. But like Peter, Parham had serious reservations about "unclean things." In other words, He didn't want to worship with people whose cultural, ethnic, and racial composite was, well, different from his own. Of course, just as God corrected Peter (Acts 10:10-16 & Galatians 2:11-21); Parham was also corrected.

A pupil of Charles Parham's student body during the Houston revival in 1905 became the instrument of God's next *corrective modification.* This young black student was excommunicated from the Second Baptist Church, which was predominantly a Black congregation. He was dis-fellowshipped for professing the holiness doctrine. Later, the young minister was invited to Los Angeles in March 1906, by Ms. Neely Terry, also an excommunicated dis-fellowshipped former member of Second Baptist Church and a student of Parham during the Houston revival. The anointed young preacher arrived in early spring 1906. Shortly thereafter, William J. Seymour became the leader of the historic Azusa revival, in the city of Los Angeles, California, from 1906 to1909. Frank Bartleman wrote an "eyewitness" account of the revival in Los Angeles in 1906, entitled; "How Pentecost Came to Los Angeles." This work was later retitled "Azusa Street."

For the last 100 years, spiritual leaders of the global community have been expostulating at length about the church's indifference to cultural, ethnic, and racial composites. Now, it's my turn to remind the church of the hostility that my great-grand parents faced when they migrated from South Carolina into the "living-space" and "pews" of those residing in Girard, Ohio.

There's still room at the cross for whomsoever desires to come – therefore, let them come! For in the words of our Lord and Savior Jesus Christ, "If you are tired from carrying heavy burdens, come to me and I will give you rest. Take the yoke I give you. Put it on your shoulders and learn from me. I am gentle and humble, and you will find rest. This yoke is easy to bear, and this burden is light" (Matthew 11: 28-30 CEV).

After centuries of loving "one's own kind," perhaps the church is finally ready to lay aside divisive differences and meaningless trivialities for the spiritual furtherance of God's Kingdom. In other words, it's time to "Reach the Hearts of People" through contemporary but effective evangelism.

REFLECTIONS

GLOSSARY

1. **Aberrant Behavior** – to change or turn away from an accepted standard or social structure.

2. **Absorption (powers other than God)** – occult power turns people away from the One who controls all things.

3. **Acquaintance** – someone who is known in a social way but who is not a close friend.

4. **Acquiesce** – to accept, agree, or allow something to happen by staying silent or by not arguing.

5. **Adulation** – excessive admiration or flattery.

6. **Aggression** – hostile or violent behavior or attitudes toward another, readiness to attack or confront, to assert one's own interests: the action of attacking without being provoked such as in the beginning a quarrel or war.

7. **Altered State of Consciousness** - (Medical definition): any of various states of awareness (as dreaming sleep, a drug-induced hallucinogenic state, or a trance) that deviate from and are usually clearly demarcated from ordinary waking consciousness.

8. **Alienate** – to cause (someone) to feel that she or he no longer belongs in a particular group, society, etc. To cause to be withdrawn or make unfriendly, hostile, or indifferent especially where attachment formerly existed.

9. **Ambivalence** – the state of having mixed feelings or contradictory ideas about something or someone.

10. **Animism** – The belief that every person, creature, and object – everything – has a soul (pg 18).

11. **Antediluvian** – made, evolved, or developed a long time ago: extremely primitive.

12. **Anti-moral** – strong opposition to social customs and codes of acceptable conduct.

13. *aposteésontai* (Greek) – depart; slide back from; giving heed to deceiving spirits or wandering spirits (Martin, Rische & Gorden, p.52).

14. **Apostasy** – blatant renunciation of or loyalty to a religious faith.

15. **Ascetic** – relating to or having a strict and simple way of living that avoids physical pleasure.

16. **Atheist** – a person who believes that God does not exist.

17. **Brainwashing** – a forcible indoctrination to induce someone to give up basic political, social, or religious beliefs and attitudes and to accept contrasting regimented ideas.

18. **Chicanery** – actions or statements that trick people into believing something that is not true: deception or trickery.

19. **Clairvoyance** – an ability to communicate with dead people, to predict future events, or to know about things that one did not actually see happen or hear about.

20. **Commune** – to communicate with someone or something in a very personal or spiritual way.

21. **Conjure** – to make (something) appear or seem to appear by using magic.

22. **Counterculture movement** – a way of life and set of attitudes opposed to or at variance with the prevailing social norms.

23. **Cult** – groups of people who share a common vision and who see themselves as separate from the rest of the world – some withdrawing literally from society, others merely withdrawing psychologically; a belief that they are different from and superior to the rest of the world while gradually developing a religion or a political entity (Appel, p. 3-4).

24. **Curtail** – reduce in extent or quantity; to impose a restriction on and deprive someone of something.

25. *daimonion* (Greek) – an evil spirit or spirits.

26. **Demonical Arts** – art or images that are inspired by demon guidance or indwelling spirit.

27. **Demons** – evil spirits that have power to enter in and out of *dimensions*. And are Satan's children; fallen angels or spirits who followed Lucifer in his rebellion against the throne of God: they worship the devil, not God (Martin, Rische & Gorden, p.52-53).

28. *didaskaliais daimonioon* (Greek) – the teaching of the demons (Martin, Rische & Gorden, p.52).

29. **Disillusionment with life** – a feeling of disappointment resulting from the discovery that something (life) is not as good as one believed it to be.

30. **Divination** – the practice of using signs (tea leaves, cards, etc.) or special powers to predict the future.

31. **Doctrine of the Demons** – is the primary denial of Jesus Christ being truly God in human flesh: or whatever leads people away from God (Martin, Rische & Gorden, p.49-64).

32. **"Double Bind"** – a distortion of one's own responses to information and to confuse different types of information based on dependency and submission: a denying of one's true feelings to appease someone else (Appel, p. 102).

33. **Eastern religions** – refers to religions originating in the Eastern world – East, South and Southeast Asia.

34. **Effacement** – to cause (something) to fade or disappear.

35. **Efflorescence** – the action or process of developing: fullness of manifestation.

36. **Egalitarianism** – a belief in human equality with respect to social, political, and economic affairs; a social philosophy advocating the removal of inequalities among people.

37. **Endemic** – growing or existing in a certain place or region: common in a particular area or field.

38. **Enlightenment** – the state of having knowledge or understanding: the act of giving someone knowledge or understanding.

39. *epagonizomai* (Greek) – to put up a stiff resistance for the faith; to struggle; to compete for a prize (Martin, Rische & Gorden, p.63).

40. **Esoteric** – requiring or exhibiting knowledge that is restricted to a small group: of special, rare, or unusual interest.

41. **Expel** – to officially force someone or something out, to leave a place, organization, or region.

42. **Familiar** – In terms of witchcraft, the familiar is the witch's partner, assisting her in various magical working including divination and spell-casting.

43. **Fatalism** – the acceptance of all things and events as inevitable; submission to fate.

44. **Flamboyant** – a person or their behavior with a tendency to attract attention because of their confidence, stylishness, lively energy or excitement.

45. **Fringe of Society** – not outlawed nor fully accepted, not subject to control by the larger or dominate society, and there is no desire to reintegrate back into the dominate society (Appel, p. 11).

46. **Furor** – an outbreak of public anger or excitement; a craze.

47. **Gnosticism** – Gnosticism a belief that salvation could be gained through knowledge (divine comprehension). The Gnostic is saved when an individual is enlightened and experiences epiphany.

48. **Gullible** – easily fooled or cheated: quick to believe something that is not true.

49. **Hedonism** – the doctrine that pleasure or happiness is the sole or chief good in life.

50. **Humanism** – a system of values and beliefs that is based on the idea that people are basically good and problems can be solved using reason instead of religion.

51. **Hypnosis** – a state that resembles sleep but in which you can hear and respond to questions or suggestions.

52. **Hysteria** – exaggerated or uncontrollable emotion or excitement, particularly among a group of people.

53. **Idealism** – the attitude of a person who believes that it is possible to live according to very high standards of behavior and honesty; a theory that the essential nature of reality lies in consciousness or reason.

54. **Identity Crisis** – a feeling of unhappiness and confusion caused by not being sure about what type of person you really are or what the true purpose of your life is.

55. **Ideology** – the set of ideas and beliefs of a group or political party.

56. **Imps** – in folklore, imps were considered smaller (lesser) demons with reduced power disguised as animals, serving as witches' familiars.

57. **Indoctrinate** – to teach (someone) to fully accept the ideas, opinions, and beliefs of a particular group and to not consider other ideas, opinions, and beliefs.

58. **Intrinsic** – belonging to a thing by its very nature.

59. **Irrational Faith** – a psychological revolt against the four formal laws of logic and the unwillingness to understand or accept time and eternity: unscientific or metaphysical (Martin, Rische & Gorden, p.23).

60. **Leitmotif** – a dominant recurring theme.

61. **Magic** – a power that allows people (such as witches and wizards) to do impossible things by saying special words or performing special actions: tricks that seem to be impossible and that are done by a performer to entertain people: special power, influence, or skill.

62. **Malevolent** – having, showing, or arising from intense often vicious ill will, spite, or hatred.

63. **Malignant (spirit-beings) forces** – forces loosed in the atmosphere causing or intending to cause harm and destruction of human beings (Martin, Rische & Gorden, p.28, 50).

64. **Maturational (developmental) Crisis** – a life crisis in which usual coping mechanisms are inadequate in dealing with a stress common to a particular stage in the life cycle or with stress caused by a transition from one stage to another.

65. **Messianic Cults** – salvation is orchestrated by a human emissary (sent on a special mission) of God, which requires total dependence upon or commitment to this individual referred to as "messiah" (Appel, p.48-53).

    a. **Conversion** – a symbolic death or "breakdown" a public manifestation of being special, singled out and a sign of "grace" (Appel, p.50).

    b. **Spiritual Marriage** – the messiah (leader) is reborn as God's Second Son, and followers are reborn as the leader's children (Appel, p.48).

    c. **Spiritual Rebirth** – a sense of purpose and revitalization and overcoming personal "demons" establishing a new identity for a messiah and followers. The messianic leader becomes a savior destined to rescue the world from imminent destruction and the followers are the chosen people who will implement their messiah's mission (Appel, p. 50).

66. **Millenarian**- a person or group of people who believe in the doctrine of the millennium (the thousand-year reign of Christ) with a longing and belief that salvation will take place on earth: a direct preparation for Judgment Day or the end of the world (Appel, p.4-5).

67. **Mind Altering** – producing mood changes (mind or behavior) or giving a sense of heightened awareness.

68. **Mirage** or **Optical phenomena** – something that is illusory: without substance or reality.

69. **Monotheism** – the doctrine or belief that there is but one God.

70. **Movement** – an organized group of people working together, to advance their shared political, social, or artistic ideas in an effort to promote or attain a desired end.

71. **Mysticism** – a religious practice based on the belief that knowledge of spiritual truth can be gained by praying or thinking deeply; the belief that direct knowledge of God, spiritual truth, or ultimate reality can be attained through subjective experience (as intuition or insight).

72. *muthos* (Greek) – fiction or mythology (Martin, Rische & Gorden, p.61).

73. **Mystery religions** – an immersion of Roman culture in the worship of multiple deities often including drunkenness and orgies, and promises salvation in the after-life (Martin, Rische & Gorden, p.51).

74. **Neurotic** – often or always fearful or worried about something: tending to worry in a way that is not healthy or reasonable.

75. **Occultism** – theory or practice: belief in or study of the action or influence of supernatural or supernormal powers.

76. **Occult paraphernalia** – objects or symbols that are used to do and/or promote a particular activity or belief system.

77. **Ominous** – suggesting that something bad is going to happen in the future.

78. **Orthodox** – accepted as true or correct by most people: supporting or believing what most people think is true: accepting and closely following the traditional beliefs and customs of a religion.

79. **Ouija board** – a device consisting of a small board on legs that rest on a larger board marked with words, letters of the alphabet, etc., and that by moving over the larger board and touching the words, letters, etc., while the fingers of spiritualists, mediums, or others rest lightly upon it, is employed to answer questions, give messages, etc.

80. **Outmoded** – no longer useful or acceptable: not modern or current.

81. **Paganism** – a religion that has many gods or goddesses, considers the earth holy, and does not have a central authority.

82. **Palmistry** – the art or activity of looking at the lines on the palms of people's hands and telling them what will happen to them in the future.

83. **Pantheistic** – a doctrine that equates God with the forces and laws of the universe: the worship of all gods of different creeds, cults, or people indifferently.

84. **Paranoia** – a serious mental illness that causes an individual to falsely believe that other people are trying to harm or do not like them.

85. **Parapsychology** - the scientific study of events that cannot be explained by what scientists know about nature and the world.

86. **Pejorative** – a word or phrase that has negative connotations or that is intended to disparage or belittle.

87. **Phenomenon** – something (such as an interesting fact or event) that can be observed and studied and that typically is unusual or difficult to understand or explain fully: someone or something that is very impressive or popular due to an unusual ability or quality.

88. **Philosophy** – the study of ideas about knowledge, truth, the nature and meaning of life, etc.

89. **Polygamy** – the state or practice of being married to more than one person at the same time (a spouse either sex may have more than one mate).

90. **Polytheism** – the doctrine of or belief in more than one god or in many gods.

91. **Possessed** – influenced or controlled by something (as an evil spirit, a passion, or an idea).

92. **Pragmatism** – a reasonable and logical way of doing things or of thinking about problems that are simply based on specific situations instead of ideas and/or theories.

93. **Professional Vigilantes** – an individual or group of people who "snatch" and forcibly detain cult members, to "deprogram" them.

94. **Proselytize** – to try to persuade people to join a religion, cause, or group: to induce someone to convert to one's faith: to recruit to a new faith or institution.

95. **Pseudoscientific** – a system of theories, assumptions, and methods erroneously regarded as being scientific.

96. **Psychic** – sensitivity to nonphysical or supernatural forces and influences: marked by extraordinary or mysterious sensitivity, perception, or understanding.

97. **Psychotic** – having or relating to a very serious mental illness that makes you act strangely or believe things that are not true.

98. *puthon* (Greek) – a spirit of divination (Martin, Rische & Gorden, p.57).

99. **Redress** – a remedy or compensation for a wrong or grievance.

100. **Reincarnation** – the idea of belief that people are born again with a different body after death.

101. **Relic** – something that is from a past time, place, culture: and object that is considered holy.

102. **Renaissance** – the activity, spirit, or time of the great revival of art, literature, and learning in Europe beginning in the 14th century and extending to the 17th century, marking the transition from the medieval to the modern world: a renewal of life, vigor, interest; rebirth or revival.

103. **Revitalization Movement** - a condemnation of modern ways, which is believed to corrupt purity (Appel, p.7).

104. **Revolution** – a forcible overthrow of a government or social order in favor of a new system.

105. **Rites** – a formal or ceremonial act or procedure customary in religious or other solemn use.

106. **Ritual** – a religious or solemn ceremony consisting of a series of actions performed according to a prescribed order; a series of actions or type of behavior regularly and invariably followed by someone.

107. **Sadistic** – enjoyment that someone gets from being violent or cruel or from causing pain.

108. **Satanism** – the worship of the Christian devil, major rituals profane the central acts of worship such as repeating the Lord's Prayer backwards, slaughtering animals to parody the crucifixion, or the sexually abusing women on the altar. The height of worship is the invocation of Satan for the working of malevolent magic (Melton, p. 108).

109. **Séance** – a meeting where people try to communicate with the spirits of dead people: a spiritualist meeting to receive spirit communications.

110. **Searchers or Seekers** – individuals or people looking for something, some magic belief or affiliation to fill up their lives: tend to have a poor sense of identity and easily become another person in as many ways as possible (Appel, p.59).

111. **"Secret or hidden Knowledge"** – oral and/or written traditions that are secretly passed down in the form of rituals, spells, and incantations from one generation to the next, also known as the occult (Martin, Rische & Gorden, p.17).

112. **Self-deification** – to exalt or position oneself as a god: to be idealized or exalted.

113. **Self-delusion** – failure to recognize reality or a belief that is not true, false idea.

114. **Self-help groups** – members share a common problem and provide mutual support to each other.

115. **Shaman** – a priest or priestess who uses magic for the purpose of curing the sick, divining the hidden, and controlling events.

116. **Shamanism** – a religious practice that involves interconnecting with natural and spiritual realms through an altered state of consciousness enabling transcendental energies to travel and communicate through parallel dimensions.

117. **Sinister** – having an evil appearance: looking likely to cause something bad, harmful, or dangerous to happen.

118. **Spiritualism** – a system of belief or religious practice based on supposed communication with the spirits of the dead, especially through mediums.

119. **Subjugation** – the process of bringing under or gaining control of (someone or something) by the use of force.

120. **Synaptic patterns** – a development in response to a set of relative information derived from an individual's life experiences and environment. The patterns are very sensitive to radical change of information received disrupts previously established synaptic patterns, resulting in changed behavior (Appel, p. 116).

121. **Symbolism** – the use of symbols to express or represent ideas.

122. **Sorceress** – (see Witch).

123. **Sorcery** – the use of magical powers that are obtained through evil spirits.

124. **Supernatural** – of or relating to an order of existence beyond the visible observable universe especially relating to God or a god, demigod, spirit, or devil.

125. **Theology** – the study of religious faith, practice, and experience: the study of God and God's relation to the world: a system of religious beliefs or ideas.

126. **Theosophy** – the teachings of a modern movement originating in the United States in 1875 and following chiefly pantheistic evolution and reincarnation.

127. **Therapeutic Cults** – salvation is framed as personal liberation (human potential) or cure through some type of affliction or payment to liberate an individual's mind and body of painful past experiences (Appel, p.19).

128. **Totalistic Cults** – attempt to control the total environment of individual followers through complete withdrawal from the world, condemning outsiders to be "satanic" or "ungodly", pressure for members to conform to the group, a strict regimented lifestyle and idea of "togetherness", a severing of all ties to the past, and requires members to give up their independent thoughts or actions (Appel, p.17).

129. **Trance** – to be in a half-conscious state characterized by an absence of response to external stimuli, typically as induced by hypnosis or entered by a medium.

130. **Utopian** – having impossibly ideal conditions especially of social organization; aiming for a state in which everything is perfect.

131. **Vulnerable** – capable of being physically or emotionally wounded: open to attack or damage.

132. **Warlock** – a man who has magical powers and practices witchcraft: a sorcerer or wizard.

133. **Wicca** – the modern religion deriving from the pre-Christian spiritual traditions of the British Isles [affirming the existence of supernatural power (as magic) and of both male and female deities who inhere in nature and that emphasizes ritual observance of seasonal and life cycles].

134. **Witch** – one that is credited with usually malignant supernatural powers; especially: a woman practicing usually black witchcraft often with the acid of a devil or familiar, esp. sorceress (2) a practitioner of Wicca (EOWC, p. 2).

135. **Witchcraft** – the practice of sorcery or black magic (2) conjuring of familiar spirits to perform feats of healing or entertainment through mediums, priestesses, sorcerers, wizards, magicians, healers, shamans and enchantresses (EOWC, p.13).

136. **Witch doctor** – a professional worker of magic usually in a primitive society, who often works to cure sickness and fight off evil spirits, curses, etc.

137. **Zoroastrianism** – a spiritual belief that the universe is a battleground of two gods that existed from the beginning. The universe is divided between their armies (EOWC, p. 30).

Bibliography

Appel, W. (1983). *Cults in America: Programmed for paradise*. New York, NY: Holt, Rinehart and Winston.

Barclay, M. T. (2011). *Beware of seducing spirits* (2nd ed.). Midland, MI: Mark Barclay Ministries.

Boa, K. D. & Bowman, R. M., Jr. (2007). *Sense & nonsense about angels & demons*. Grand Rapids, MI: Zondervan.

Evans, T. (2005). *The truth about angels and demons*. Chicago, IL: Moody Publishers.

F + W Media, Inc. (2016). *The beginner's guide to divination*. Avon, MA: Adams Media.

Hexham, I., & Poewe, K. (1986). *Understanding cults and new religions*. Grand Rapids, MI: William B. Eerdmans Publishing Company.

Hopkins, S. (2002). *The cult of Jabez: And the falling away of the church in America*. Burnet, TX: Bethel Press.

Illes, J. (2014). *Encyclopedia of witch craft: The complete a-z for the entire magical world*. New York, NY: Harper One.

Martin, W., Rische, J. M., & Gorden, K. V. (2008). *The kingdom of the occult: From the author of the kingdom of the cults.* Nashville, TN: Thomas Nelson.

Melton, J. G. (1992). *Encyclopedic handbook of cults in America: Revised and updated edition.* New York, NY: Garland Publishing, Inc.

Merriam-Webster. (2015). Dictionary and Thesaurus. Retrieved from http://www.merriam-webster.com/

Murphy, E. (2003). *The handbook for spiritual warfare*. Nashville, TN: Thomas Nelson, Inc.

Raupert, J. G. (2015). *The new black magic: And the truth about the Ouija-board*. London, England, UK: Forgotten Books.

Reese, W. L. (1980). *Dictionary of philosophy and religion: Eastern and western thought.* Highlands, N.J.: Humanities Press Inc.

Safra, J. E. & Aguilar-Cauz, J. (2006). *Britannica Encyclopedia of world religions*. Chicago, IL: Encyclopedia Britannica, Inc.

Unger, M. F. (1971). *Demons in the world today: A study of occultism in the light of God's word.* Wheaton, IL: Tyndale House Publishers.

Whyte, H. A. M. (1989). *Demons & deliverance* (2nd ed.). New Kensington, PA: Whitaker House.

Wright, H. N. (2011). *The complete guide to crisis & Trauma counseling: What to do and say when it matters most.* Ventura, CA: Regal.

WWW.DrGlennWalter.Com

Leadership Training Consultants, Ltd.
6500 Emerald Parkway
Suite 100
Dublin, Ohio 43016
614-493-8543

Made in United States
Orlando, FL
08 January 2023